It's Decision Time!

365 Days of Sarcasm, Success and Strategies for You To Make More Money

By Suzanne Evans

Suzanne Evans

P.O. Box 1089

Murrells Inlet, SC 29576

866-496-3060

support@helpmorepeople.com

www.suzanneevans.org

Limits of Liability and Disclaimer of Warranty

Warning – Disclaimer

ISBN 978-1-937170-00-4

If you want to make fast decisions, more money, and make a difference visit www.suzanneevans.org for tons of free information, resources, and tools.

About Suzanne

Suzanne Evans, owner and founder of Suzanne Evans Coaching, LLC, is the tell-it-like-it-is, no fluff boss of business building. She supports, coaches, and teaches over 30,000 women enrolled in her wealth and business building programs. Having surpassed the seven figure mark herself in just over three years, she's coached her private clients to total revenues exceeding 8 million dollars. This year she will launch her Global Impact Project, a not for profit serving women worldwide in education, entrepreneurship, and equality.

For Larry. . . . He didn't change my life. He just reminded me I could change my life.

To any person who ever wanted to launch a
business, buy a business, build a business, or start
a business, and knew it would take fast decisions to
make it work. Hell yeah!

Preface

This book is real stuff, about real things that get real results. I did not intend it to make you feel good. I intended for it to piss you off enough that you will start making a decision. I intended for it to make you more money and get you what you want in life.

I think far too many people encourage others to take their time and find their path. I am very clear that our time here is limited and our opportunities come and go. I want this book to create urgency and clarity for you. It won't always feel good, but it will get you moving. It will force you to decide.

I realize you may not like me before you read this book, while you read it, or after you read it. I am OK with that. I am not OK with being nice so you feel better. I am not OK with being soft so we can both feel better. I may not even know you, but I can tell you that I believe in you. I know your circumstances are not your possibility and that you have something to offer. I know that a fun, meaningful, wealthy life is your birthright, but I also know you earn it.

Nobody is going to hand you anything. You have to claim it.

Follow and implement these ideas for the next 365 days and you won't recognize your life. How do you want to live? How much money do you want to make? How do you want to spend your time? You can have whatever you work for. It's decision time!

Love,

Suzanne

It's Decision Time!

Day 1

I don't need you to like me.

I don't need you to listen to me.

You need to listen.

And to hell with liking me.

Day 2

Let me just spill the beans for you... business success has almost nothing to do with business know-how and everything to do with mindset. The marketing pieces can be learned, and sometimes you can even delegate small parts of them out, but the deep core belief that it takes to manifest a BIG business is your central key to success. **You can think what you want, but if your business dream is not where you had imagined it would be, all the details in the world will not push you through to business success.** I know because I have tried it. I have tried to do everything right and get all my marketing ducks in a row, but if my belief about what is possible for me was out of alignment, all those tools just sat there. Nothing much happened.

Day 3

Poverty doesn't make you more virtuous.

It just makes you **more broke.**

Day 4

Sometimes you have to do things old school and learn the hard way. I'm a perfect example of that. In the beginning I worked really hard to create a business, and **before I knew it I just had another job.**

I was only working with one-on-one clients, it's hard work, and every dollar I made was dependent on those hours. When I shifted that model and offered other products and programs that didn't have to involve me it made a huge difference.

Day 5

Stop resisting sales as evil.

Embrace it as the most powerful engine of transformation.

Day 6

Sales in NOT a four-letter word.

Go ahead ... count 'em!

Day 7

I am all for making a massive difference.

But I am also **for making a massive profit** at the same time.

Day 8

I really come from a marketing mindset, which is to build a coaching business as apposed to just a practice. **A real coaching business has multiple streams of income.** It means one-on-one coaching, groups, or you may have an associate coach that's leading some programs for you. Also, this includes products like books and ezines, audio programs and DVDs.

This means programs you lead once live and then you record those to be sold at a later time. Building a coaching business can also include workshops, seminars, and having all different types of clients from VIP platinum level clients at higher rates to lower level packages.

Day 9

The formula for success:

Passion

+

Tenacity

+

No Excuses

=

Success!

Day 10

Please don't judge people, places or opportunities of the correctness to sale. **You will be surprised where people will find you and where you can find people.** You share your messages and gifts where you can and don't judge opportunities (especially in the beginning) – just get your message out!

Day 11

If you choose excuses and blame over action **you will stay stuck.**

Day 12

This could be the day that **money** stops being the enemy.

And becomes your best friend.

Day 13

The only reason you will not succeed is because of the story you are telling yourself. **I wish you could see YOU from the view I have.** All the hope, possibilities, brilliance, power and talent. Take that image and use it for the fuel to do your best work. You can not help more people living in the "what if's" and "maybe's." What will your new thoughts be?

Day 14

I don't have the time to pitter around.

And neither do you.

We have lives to change.

Day 15

If you choose **what's wrong** over what's possible **it will be impossible.**

Day 16

Simply "Be" ... and the universe rewards you with abundance.

How is that working for you?

Day 17

I knew that **connecting with people in person** is the most powerful way to build and grow a business, to get my message heard, and to help more people.

Day 18

Living **your mission** is more than having people like you.

It is insuring folks who need you find you.

Day 21

The more money you make, the more you make your own dreams (and the dreams of others) come true.

Day 22

The more money you make the more secure you are. **And the more you can give that security to others.**

Day 23

One of the rules in business & life: **Do it how you said you would do it** — don't half ass anything.

Day 24

I expect A LOT from my clients. I expect them to show up in their lives in huge ways and bust their butt building their business because when they don't, the people they can help don't get served. I remind them of that standard, I hold them to that standard, and I do not waiver even when I want to. I owe that to them.

Day 25

Start filling **YOUR bank account**
(instead of someone else's)

Day 26

In this world of technology, gadgets, and high-tech **the pendulum is swinging back to** face-to-face relationship based marketing.

Day 27

Stop wishing for profits. Hoping for profits. And actually **start taking them to the bank.**

Day 28

You do know that sales doesn't have **two horns, a tail and a pitchfork** don't you?

Day 29

No matter your background, experiences, or outlook, **you've been selling successfully your entire life!**

Day 30

Your rate is your announcement to the world of your **confidence in your skill set.**

Day 31

Offer a freebie! Do you have something on your website that really shows the best of what you do and offer and it is free? This is a great way for people to have an initial interaction with you and want more. Remember KLT Factor: Know. Like. Trust. Your potential clients need to feel as if you understand them and have a solution to their problems. Have a wonderful and content rich freebie to do just that.

Day 32

When **your talent, skill or gift** can transform someone else's life, sales becomes all about making a difference.

Day 33

No moment is more "sacred" than when **your prospect chooses to invest** in the highest possible vision for their lives.

Day 34

The fastest, least expensive **path to their dreams** runs directly through your business.

Day 35

Your clients connect to you most **when you are vulnerable, genuine, and consistent.** Your style becomes your signature and that is what makes people want more from you. I am not perfect... I have a mixed up combo of sweet and saucy, but it is all me, all the time. What is your style... you can find that style just by noticing when you are in complete flow and don't even have to think about your next move.

Day 36

Essentials for life:

Air

Water

Love

...and

Sales

Not the "S" word you expected?

Day 37

If you're bored, broke, or confused you need to ask people to work with you. No one can be negative and serving at the same time.

Day 38

I think there are a lot of people saying they are serial entrepreneurs and they aren't so serial- just sayin!

Day 39

Business is numbers.

Do you know yours?

Look at your numbers everyday, **study them, and they will go up!**

Day 40

You don't need the money until you make the decision. You can not build a business based on where you are-- only where you are going!

Day 41

You can **intend** until the cows come home, but it takes more than that to get to 7 **figures.**

Day 42

Meditation is great, but it's **hard to make sales from the lotus position.**

Day 43

I'm willing to be the boogie woman! If it **gets you off your ass** to discover the **REAL reasons your business isn't working.**

Day 44

Are you a BO or a HO?

Biz Owners (BO) invest, take risks, and do whatever it takes. Hobbyist Owners (HO) **love to dream and believe**, but don't take massive action. Which are you?

Day 45

Isn't it interesting to see people that **the pain of a monthly payment is stronger** than the pain of not getting the strategy / support / direction they need. No business man or woman is an island.

Day 46

Have a point of view and be unapologetic. Tonight someone left my call because I was "ranting" and said pissed... Cool. I am proud of my style and point of view...what's yours? Mine is work hard, don't complain, and be more about making a difference than being liked. Yours?

Day 47

Hell Yeah!

Day 48

Don't get a cheap coach.

OK, do I have to say anything else? Seems obvious — **cheap gets you cheap.** Ever think — if this coach is so good why do they charge so little? You should.

Day 49

Don't get cheap business cards.

I always forget my biz cards... (ick — I know!) But if you are going to have them, **have them say expensive!**

Day 50

Don't go networking or speaking in cheap clothes.

I cannot tell you how many smart, savvy, fun people I meet who while they are speaking to me I am totally distracted by the fact that they look as if they have put absolutely no effort in showing up as their best self. I don't pretend to be a fashionista — BUT I want to look my best, feel my best, and show up as my best self.

Day 51

Don't be cheap with your resources.

Give away your best and they will buy the rest. Seriously! I hate when people tease you in the attempt to make more money. If you stand by your services, are great at what you do, and love people up, they will want more. Don't be cheap.

Day 52

Don't be cheap with your time.

Business takes effort. When I hear people say they don't want to work hard I am clear on their best path. **Get a job.** Business takes hustle and if you love what you do it won't feel like work. Being cheap with your time will get you cheap results.

Day 53

Know the definition of business

The definition of business is: *Economic system in which goods and services are exchanged for one another or money, on the basis of their perceived worth. Every business requires some form of investment and a sufficient number of customers to whom its output can be sold at profit on a consistent basis.*

Business is profit. Business is not to make you feel good, others feel good, build community, or otherwise — it is great when it does those things. That is a side effect and a beautiful one, but when you put those above profit you will struggle. You will make this hard and you will go broke. Profit first — then all the other missions.

Day 54

Don't throw like a girl.

There is a lot of feminine energy talk these days. I am all for feminine energy and masculine energy and all energies, but don't let it be your primary message. **People want results. They want a plan.** They need to pay their bills, lose weight, get clients, or be happy. Talk results; not concepts.

Day 55

Be pissed off regularly.

If you are still reading this you may not hate me — yet. But I get pissed off a lot and in a good way. **I use that to teach, to share, and to stop people from making the same mistakes I did.** Use your opinions — don't hide them. People need more truth in business.

Day 56

Get real or go home.

This is business. This is entrepreneurship and it's not for the faint of heart. It is not for everybody and frankly, many people I meet should not go into business. They can have a big impact on the world in multiple ways, but being a business owner is not their best path. **Be serious. Be ready. Be willing. Be committed.** Business is one of the most beautiful (and scary) journeys you will ever take. Get real or go home.

Day 57

We've been trained as coaches that the client always leads the conversation. **If the client were meant to lead every single conversation, they wouldn't need to come to you.** They would already know the answers.

Day 58

Ask for money: **Your gift is your gift because you are meant to share it and be rewarded,** and those rewards are meant for your abundance and generosity to others.

Day 59

Stop confusing giving back with giving it away. **When you give your services away you don't help anyone.** You lose the value and the opportunity to create revenue that you can use to contribute.

Day 60

Let go of the shame. **God did not intend for us to be broke or worry about money.** Just look at the Universe... the blade of grass does not struggle to grow. The environment is abundant with air to breathe. Money worry is a choice. You always get what you need when you need it.

Day 61

Make it a priority to make as much money as you absolutely can. **And then be armed and ready to change your world and the world around you.** I am motivated to educate girls. I am motivated to cultivate entrepreneurs. I am committed to bringing equality. It will take money, so I am fine with making more and making it a focus.

Day 62

Sacrifice. My definition of sacrifice is doing something you have never done to get something you have never had. Sacrifice is not giving something up, it is doing something more.

Day 63

Stop blaming. If you want success you have to take 100% responsibility for every single part of your life.

Day 64

Lack vs. Life. People do not attract lack. God is good all the time. God does not send lack to people. **People attract life not lack.** Life is a series of hiccups, imperfections, and traumas. That happens to everyone evenly. What you do with it and how you react to it creates your destiny.

Day 65

Give up on the miracle. No one is going to discover you, rush to give you a TV show, make you rich, and save you from having to get clients. Sorry to kill the dream. **YOU are your miracle.** Do the marketing. Master the mindset. Take the action. That is the miracle.

Day 66

Broke is a Joke. Oh... this one is going to sting for some of you.
Here goes (all in love). If you are broke building a business for you will be a joke. Everyone must finance their dream. I sold things on Ebay and worked 60 hours a week; some clients used credit cards; Sly Stone sold his wife's rings. If you are broke with no plan or desire to make money to finance mentoring and your business you are on the hallucination train. Get off, get a job, and finance your business.

Day 67

Prioritize the truth. This is where gas, groceries, and coaching come in. I know you have to eat (believe me, I love to eat) and I know we all have basic needs, but **the truth is if you can barely afford gas money then you are not prioritizing the truth.** Truth is that we live in an abundant Universe where all our financial needs are met as easily as air. But, it does take a decision. It does take the commitment to doing whatever it takes to do both — gas/groceries and coaching.

Day 68

Ask how bad? How bad do you want it? How important is it to you? Failure is not an option which means sleep, time, money, skill set, weight, race, sex, sexual orientation, appearance, disability, and education will not keep me from my business. How bad do you want this? I recently met a multi-millionaire who came from nothing. He said he used to have to decide between groceries and business growth. **He said he learned to eat off of $15 a week because he was hungrier for his dream than for food.**

Day 69

Whatever you have committed to honor it at all costs. Whether that commitment was made to yourself or someone else. **Lie enough to yourself and others and nothing you say will hold weight.** Do what you say you will do.

Day 70

Don't be late (literally and figuratively) and if you are, don't make excuses. **Do it when you say you will.** No one wants to work with someone unpredictable. Period.

Day 71

Don't half ass anything. The way you show up and deliver is the exact way you will increase your revenue and your lifestyle.

Day 72

Don't be cheap and tell yourself you are frugal — stay in a nice place, tip well, fly first class, give to others, invest deeply in yourself.

Day 73

When you act in desperation you get desperate results.

Strategy

Responsibility

Action

in that order.

Can I get a hell yeah?

Day 74

Balance does not equal procrastination — all the time I hear I will not work that hard, I will not go that far or that long because I want to maintain balance. Don't fool yourself into thinking that doing less is balance. **The most balanced people I know are really hard workers.** They do what they love — many for 10-12 hours a day. They have great support, they delegate the things they hate, and they play harder than they work. Balance is joy. Balance is not how hard you do or do not work.

Day 75

If you want to change the world, **start by changing your world.**

Day 76

You start **making money** when you stop caring what people think.

Day 77

We are responsible *to* our clients, not *for* our clients.

And there are two messages here for us. Most of us are coaches, teachers or healers AND we are clients to someone. We are not responsible for the success or failure of others and no coach, mentor, or teacher will ever be responsible for the success of US. And this is where it can get into some pretty tricky marketing waters... you see all of us share our client triumphs and testimonials as celebrations and announcements to the world to market our services, but the truth is...

Every person is 100% responsible for their success and failures.

Day 78

You do it afraid.

The truth is:

If you are afraid — you have company.

The prescription is:

Do it anyway.

Day 79

Life is unpredictable.

All your plans will change.

You will fail.

And you can get back up.

Day 80

When in doubt, hold your hand up in front of you. Look at your fingertips. No one else has those. Only you. Remember there is no competition. There is no comparison. There is only YOU. Look straight ahead.

Day 81

There are people who don't know what you do. **Tell them!**

Day 82

Wherever you are is **where you are.**

Day 83

Don't be afraid to be yourself. If they don't like you, they aren't your people.

Day 84

You are in the **business of collecting names.**

Day 85

Give away your best stuff and they'll buy the rest.

Day 86

The way you do your newsletters **is the way you're running your business.**

Day 87

Clear out the clutter. Money is energy and it must have space to travel. Some ways it does NOT travel well: through stacks of paper, piles of clothes, or disorganized and unused files. Find huge chunks of open space and air for all the good stuff to come in. And no excuses...if this simple thought overwhelms you or scares the heck out of you, contact a personal organizer.

Day 88

Marketing alone does not work.

You need to

be authentic,

be effective,

and

change the world.

Day 89

You can help anybody in the world, but you can't help everybody. You need to pick who you want to work with and who can pay you!

Day 90

If you have no free time **how will you build your business?**

Day 91

Before you can have passive income **you need to get active income.** You can't serve millions until you serve one.

Day 92

Everything you write (web page, etc) should be a map guiding people to where you want them to go.

Day 93

Authority inspires!

Day 94

Most people shop from coach to coach so long they don't need a coach because the situation has become so desperate. **Decide swiftly, so your business can grow swiftly.**

Day 95

Don't do what's cute – do what sells.

Day 96

Everything is easier if you remember who you are. ~Suzanne's Mom & Dad

Day 97

GO change the world, but start by changing yours. **If you are waiting to be perfect, you are actually keeping people from an experience of learning from you now** and just the way you are. Your flaws are your relevance and your obstacles are your guide posts to success. Stop cursing the pain of growth and change. Start celebrating that you can feel it and that you are living it. If in this moment you are comfortable then you aren't stretching big enough.

Day 98

Stop competing. There is no competition. **You are as unique as your fingerprints, so unless you have been cloned you live daily in a competition free zone.** Be you, deliver value, and ignore the idea of competition.

Day 99

Stop resisting. What do you know you need to do next? Get support, let go of a client, make a plan, or change your life? **What we resist becomes our shield to attract clients and income.** Release the resistance and release the wall between you and income.

Day 100

Stop pretending. There's a lot of exaggeration that goes on out there. People think if you have a certain house, car, or life you will be more attractive. **Want to know what is highly attractive? Being YOU!** Stop pretending and start delivering the uniqueness of you.

Day 101

Stop struggling. It truly is optional to make this hard and ugly. There is help, ideas, and support everywhere you turn. There is always your free will. You always have a choice. You can choose to make it hard or make it simple. (I would go with simple — have done hard).

Day 102

Stop gossiping. Yep– the truth is most of us never left high school. We still grab the phone and share the latest news or judgment we have about someone. It takes less energy to love than to judge. The more you support others, the more you will succeed.

Day 103

Stop worrying. Somebody is gonna hate you – they just will. Someone will think you are foolish or maybe even crazy, but there will also be the people you save. There will be the people you heal and the people you transform. I think you should focus on them instead.

Day 104

Stop wavering. Make a decision. You don't need the money, time, or resources until you decide to do something. You know right now that there is something you need to do and you keep processing, pondering, and thinking. Make a decision and every opportunity you need will come forth. Isn't that cool?

Day 105

Be yourself and your business will grow.

Day 106

Your movement is the single most important element in your business. Is yours clear? Are you ready? What will you change? Stop marketing and start a movement.

Day 107

We **always have the money** to do the
things we REALLY want to do.

Day 108

When I was growing my business I:

Found a mentor that was patient, loving, and kind — she told me what to do... I did it 100% and grew my business to over six figures.

Next, I worked with a **marketing master** and did the same. Even in fits of frustration I did everything he said and grew my business to over $300,000.

Finally, I worked with my current mentor and again, **I humbly agreed** to be the best follower to ever be doing exactly what he suggested and I earned **7 figures** in revenue.

Day 109

What I have learned is most people would rather be **right than rich.** They would rather ask questions than obediently take action. Are you doing all that is asked of you by your coach and mentor — and I don't mean most — I mean EVERYTHING? Because it takes 100% commitment to follow and take action on exactly what they share has worked for them. **Why would you work with someone and then not take their advice and direction?** What does it say about you that you invest (or don't invest at all) and then ignore the information?

Day 110

Sell first. Create Second. I know this feels backwards, but what is the point of spending hours, months, and energy creating something that does not yet have an audience? Yes, you should have an outline, a time frame, and a vision, but let go of the details like the space or the delivery or the HOW. When you get people investing in your services the how will reveal itself and everything you need, will appear. It will.

Day 111

Focus on direct relationship marketing if you are looking for more cash flow. There is a lot we could be doing like tweaking our sites, adding more elements of social media, finishing our book, etc. BUT if you need to increase your revenue quickly, ONLY focus on the marketing that will have direct results in income. (Having intro sessions, speaking at events, emailing/contacting joint ventures, following up with clients from the past, and re-connecting with people that have shown an interest in your services.)

Day 112

Do not do it alone. Get help or support. If you are wondering why you are not making enough or have enough clients yet and you are doing everything yourself, that is one big AH-ha! I recommend you outsource some of the day-to-day administrative tasks to a virtual assistant. The details are all a distraction! Delegate them!

Day 113

Stop, breathe, and believe. We usually get fixated on details because it is easier than marketing.

Yep.

See... I know the truth! When you cannot seem to get out of the planning process stop, take a breath, and ask yourself what are you avoiding? What is the fear? Check in with a buddy or a coach to burst through that belief!

Day 114

Help More People. **The perfect color, location, program, or detail does not help more people.** It is important to make your services and offerings first class, organized, and professional, but these details are not what change people's lives. The moment when they invest in themselves is where your client begins to change and shift. Work towards that moment and the delivery of your work will be automatic. I know you... you would never not deliver, follow through, or help someone. Help More People. You do that through marketing and sharing your services not through the details.

Day 115

Honor your Commitments

In business your commitment is your word. Be on time, be ready, and over deliver. I have actually had a coach who did not show up for calls. Now, we all make a mistake, but follow through, show up, and deliver. If you have a product going out, be certain it goes out on time. If you are delivering a service, make certain it is as promised. You may glass these over as obvious, but stop and think. Am I honoring every commitment at the absolute highest level?

Day 116

Set an Example

I read a great quote the other day... *"Your sermon is best told by your life and not your lips."* Make certain you are modeling the positive image for your business and services. **Your appearance, presence, energy, and language all represent YOU.** It is easy to get busy in the day to day and forget what we are sharing. Sometimes it can be the smallest thing that someone picks up on and that is the image they carry forever. Preach through your actions and your words.

Day 117

Run it Like a Business

When you are in the service industry, the same best practices business rules apply. You **do not avoid policies, efficiencies, and procedures** because your business is helping and supporting others. To truly help and support, you run your business clean and clear. Have policies, have your team and your clients understand them, and have them in writing. Keep all conversations and communication on a business level and remind yourself why you are running this business. If you are here to serve, then make sure your business is serving everyone's highest interest by being clear and being well informed.

Day 118

Have a Mentor

When you have a seasoned person to ask for guidance and support, everything is easier. One of my mentors always says, "Business is messy" and it can be, so to have someone to sound board, ask, and advise is leveraging your best interests in business growth. I am telling you... MENTORS... I **don't leave home without them.**

Day 119

Be Uncomfortable

Change is good. **Not always easy. Not always comfortable,** but it means something is shifting and we are moving. Being uncomfortable in your business and stretching yourself beyond the comfort zone means you are NOT in hobby mode. Begin to worry if everything is perfect and you are care free! It is in the discomfort that we risk, journey, and leap!

Day 120

Your gifts are unique and only you can share the blessing of you. Make sure you are in wealth conscious business mode. It will serve you, serve your clients, serve your success, and serve your income growth.

Day 121

Have a clear vision of exactly what you want – **relationship, money, freedom, environment, and spiritual.** If you have a clear vision in writing and in your view, it is harder to let that vision go or the dream die.

Day 122

Get real. One of my mentors says... *"It is simple, but it is not easy."* **Success is hard work.** No one ever won the Oscar, Gold Medal, Nobel Peace Prize, or Fortune 500 by half ass showing up. And don't fool yourself... are you thinking you are working hard or are you spending a lot of time around thinking about succeeding and processing your next step?

Day 123

Get good advice. The people around me won't let me quit. I have surrounded myself with a circle of influence. I have a tribe of tough and loving go-getters. A friend and coach emailed me last week and said – **"hold fast- we need your confidence. Don't stop."** That made me cry as I was reminded people were depending on me.

Day 124

I know you have gifts to share.
Your life experience has value and people
are meant to be transformed by your
connection and your talent. Care enough to
keep going. Care enough to share and keep
going.

Day 125

If you do what you love and you love people while you do it, there is no reason to quit. **Stopping is not an option.** See you at the finish line!

Day 126

Just because I am a coach it doesn't mean I am responsible for you to show up, work hard, or succeed. We actually have people ask us to refund them for a program if they did not use it. This is not Wal-Mart. I want every one of you to have a refund policy and stick by it and stick to it. All businesses have policies and because we "help" people does not mean it is our responsibility to have someone show up for a call or open a notebook. I did my part. I created the product and delivered the program — clients have to do theirs. There are no refunds for being lazy.

Day 127

What you really want is to be asking yourself what can I do to reach my fullest potential today and **how can I help others reach theirs?**

Day 128

If you have to say you are conscious — you may not be.

There is a lot of conscious entrepreneur talk going around. It's never a good idea to fly your "conscious" flag. How about work hard, make lots, give back, and let others call you conscious? Focus on the goal: **to have a profitable business.** Conscious is a title you get — not one you give yourself. If you use your money to make a difference in your life and others, you will be more than conscious.

Day 129

You have to invest to make a business work. From day one **I spent money in and on** my business. I worked two jobs to do it. You can decide where it comes from, but you better have a financial foundation for your business.

1) day job;
2) loan;
3) credit;
4) spouse support;
5) current revenue; and
6) savings.

Have a plan to SPEND money in your business. It takes investment.

Day 130

You aren't really in business if you aren't selling. **The transformation is actually IN the sale.** I know many people are really concerned about feeling pushy, hard, or aggressive. There is one easy key that makes sales fun, easy, and profitable – LOVE!

Day 131

Sales is something you do **for people and not something you do to people.** You have gifts to share and in those gifts you have the "answer" or "solution" people need for their pain. If you don't make the decision to love your clients and prospects then you can't help them. Most people say their dream is not based in money, but meaning, helping, and serving. I agree! But you can only help people in a limited way if you are not asking for the sale.

Day 132

Remember why do you do what you do?

Are you really here to give back?

Giving back means **giving people the opportunity to invest in themselves** and grow.

Day 133

The more you keep your values intact, **the more successful you will be at selling.**

Day 134

There is honor and strength in asking for money. In other words having people pay for your services gives them skin in the game and there is no better investment in the world than the investment in you. Don't take that opportunity away from clients.

Day 135

The time is now. YOUR job is to get
potential clients to make a decision – not to
say yes. Just remember that **not
everyone is meant to work with
you,** but the most difficult thing for people
to do is decide. You have to hold the space
for that. Whether the answer is a **hell yes**
or a **hell no** ... love them to a decision.

Day 136

With love and caring for people you can make more money and a bigger difference. What beliefs do you lead WITH? Do you believe your mission is to help people? Do you believe that by selling you serve? Do you believe selling is nothing more than sharing? Notice the beliefs you lead with.

Day 137

Think about changing your sales language and next time you have a sales call or conversation say – **I am going to love them to the YES!** Selling is nothing more than love. And I know this is why you do what you do to love people so that love gets paid forward. So, love people and watch your world and their world transform all through the SALE.

Day 138

There is no competition. People often come up to me and say that they really want to do something but that there are so many other people already doing it, that they aren't sure if it's what they should do.

What people forget quite frequently is that there can only be one YOU!

Day 139

Do you know how many marketing and mindset coaches there are out there?

There are hundreds, if not thousands, if not tens of thousands of them out there – but there is no one doing it like me.

There is no one else doing it "Help More People" style. Likewise, no one can do what you do like you can.

Let go of the idea of competition. There is no competition. The only competition you will find is a manufactured competition that you have created.

Day 140

Don't wait for everything to be "just right" to launch a product or to even start your business. This kind of perfectionism holds people back from helping people, making money, and really making a difference in the world.

There's a great Marianne Williamson quote that says, **"Your playing small doesn't serve the world."** It also doesn't serve your family, your spouse, or your church, or your community, or your friends.

Day 141

I often hear people saying "I would do this, but I have to take care of my 95 year old mother," or "I would do this but I have three toddlers at home," and many other excuses beginning with "I would do this but..."

By playing small, not being in the right mindset, not asking for clients, not marketing yourself, or putting all the pieces together, you are being a terrible example for your children, community, family, friends, etc. **When you are a leader and you step up and build a business that makes a difference in this world,** you change everyone's mindset, and indeed you change the world.

Day 142

So many people want to change the world, but fail to realize that the only person they can directly change is themselves. **You must start with your own mindset.** Your sales conversions, your ability to make money, whether or not you are comparing yourself to others or not, and any uncertainty that you're experiencing are all reflections of your belief in what is possible for you.

Day 143

When I decided to get my **"mind set"** in the right direction – *notice that I used two words,* **mindset** *is really about getting your* **mind set** *in the right way* – everything started to come together for me. Treat your belief in yourself like a thermostat and not a thermometer. You set it where you want it to be.

Day 144

People always want to know how I did it and what **the one big shift was** that happened.

It's simple.

I didn't stop. I didn't stop when:

* People said No. * I ran out of money.
* I got tired. * I went dry creatively.
* Someone hurt my feelings. * Someone no showed. * People discouraged me.
* I felt I wasn't enough. * I was told I wasn't enough. * The clients I did have left. * No one new came. * The car broke down. * A family member died.
* I was confused. * I was scared.

I didn't stop!

Day 145

Tenacity. The only business skill you ever need to know.

Day 146

When the money runs out... Get a job! (I like to call it a business loan) Fund your dream...if you believe in it enough, **find the income stream to support it.**

Day 147

When people leave... Find new people! Clients leave for a reason. They are often afraid of success and some leave because they are complete. Let them go, take a breath, and ASK – find new people to share your message. Don't stop.

Day 148

When you are scared... Go through it!
The only way out is through. There
is no magic pill. There is no step-by-step
system for fear. When you do it – it gets
easier... when you build that muscle you get
braver. Courage is a learned skill.

Day 149

When you get tired... Ask for help! No man is an island. I didn't build this alone and neither can you. You need to only work in your brilliance and delegate the rest.

Day 150

When someone hurts your feelings... Remember who you are! I didn't get in this business to make friends. **I do this to make a difference.** Not everyone will like me, my style, or my methods. There are other coaches for them. I know who I am.

Day 151

When you feel you aren't enough... Know the truth. You are a child of God. You are here to let your light shine and you are enough. If you are reading this, it means **you believe in possibility.** Share that possibility for it is love.

Day 152

Listen. Many business owners keep selling (or pushing) their products/services and they are not awakened to the fact that people have changed, especially in the last year, and want different things. There is a different need and desire to make lasting change and **if you just sell and do not listen** you are not aiming to make a difference. Ask your clients what they want most and also pay close attention to what is not said. **You cannot make money selling what you think people need** – listen to what they want and be ready to change, adapt, or grow.

Day 153

Get Live! The technology gauntlet has swung. There are so many x-boxes, ipad touches, tweets, and texts that **people are starving for human contact.** How can you connect with people one-on-one? There is no better way to make that deep connection and find out how you can help people. Plan a time to take people to lunch, host drinks at an event you are attending, do a one day event, find a local expo – and networking, networking, networking always works when you work it. **Live and in person IS THE NEW social networking trend.**

Day 154

Pick up the phone! The best (please hear me out on this one) **BEST way to close sales and get clients right now is picking up the phone and speaking to people.** You must make a connection and ASK for the sale. Take 100% responsibility for your offerings and for helping people. If you are looking to fill a program or get clients put on a kitchen timer for 15 minutes, brainstorm a list of 25 people, then pick up the phone, show them how you can help, and ASK for the sale. Don't hide behind your computer ~ connect and ask!

Day 155

You don't have to have the answer! You just need to be clear about asking.

Day 156

I had a need to be right for a long time. Maybe about 30 years – it kept me in a job I hated, my max earning was about $50k, I had no free time, and had created a situation where I could hardly make any of my own decisions. It became clear to me that **being right no longer served me.** I went as far as to have the belief that I wasn't really interested in seeking therapy or coaching. Period. I realize I was deeply afraid they might make me "wrong".

Day 157

Yes, but. Just remove it from your vocabulary. I have my private clients take an improv class, because the #1 rule of improv is YES! Start changing the "Yes, but" to "YES, YES!" "Yes, but" will keep you stuck in your excuses around time, money, and knowledge.

REFRAME: YES! YES! Anything worth doing is worth doing poorly to start with!

Day 158

I quit. This is always the easiest answer. It can be quick and it gets you out of pain – fast! But, guess what? Nothing changes...

REFRAME: I get exactly what I need when I need it. Is quitting going to move me closer to my dreams?

Day 159

I didn't get what I needed. Blame is evil. I know – I did it. It makes us feel better when it isn't out fault. But again, it doesn't move us forward or change our outcomes.

REFRAME: I am 100% responsible for everything that happens – good, bad or in between.

Day 160

There isn't enough (Time, Money, Resources, Help). When we are working from lack we get lack.

REFRAME: Everything I need is already present. And there is more than enough.

Day 161

That hurt my feelings or **I don't like how that made me feel.** Feelings are choices, so when we choose hurt or negativity we then send that energy out into a ripple effect through the world.

REFRAME: I choose how I feel about everything. No one can make me feel anything. That is my choice. So, if I am offended the offense is within me.

Day 162

Not listening. Many of you are working with coaches or in programs, but not willing to really do what is required of you or fully listen to their guidance.

REFRAME: I have chosen this person or this path for a reason and I am willing to do what is required even if I don't understand how or it might make me wrong.

Day 163

When we step up to self-responsibility in all we do, we eliminate the need to be right. We eliminate the fear of sacrifice. To truly help more people you have to be willing to help yourself. To be the change in the world, you have to change. **And it starts with being ok with letting go.** If we can let go of being right and not care who gets the credit then we can change the world over and over and over again.

Day 164

Stop basing your value and your success on what's coming into your inbox. Shut it down, put it in a filter, and go build your business. Go tell people about your story, share your message, and share your movement. **The minute you begin to compare yourself to others,** or you look to others for validation, it will slow you down and the phone will stop ringing.

Day 165

The answer that no one wants to hear is that there is no magic pill! The way to build a successful, sustainable business is to **start talking** to one person, and then you **talk** to two people, and then you **talk** to those people about how they can **talk** to someone.

Day 166

Nothing gets built offline or online unless you take the time, the energy, and the commitment to make connection after connection after connection.

Day 167

The wonderful quote, "Be more interested than interesting" is relevant to this. The worst thing in the world is to do when making connections or partaking in any kind of marketing activities like social media is to say something like, **"Hi, I'm Suzanne! Buy my stuff!" Nobody cares!**

Walk into every room (or virtual event, or social media) like it's your party. What would you do if it were your party? You would thank people for coming. You would ask them how they are. You would see what you could do for them. You would be more interested than interesting.

Day 168

I often get told that someone is waiting to start their business or one of my programs or make a change when the time is right. Without being disrespectful, it is laughable.

Laughable for a few reasons:

First, to believe that we are actually in that much control.

Second, to believe that there is anything more than just a delay in your destiny is out of integrity.

And third, if you have thought it even for a nanosecond then the time is now.

Day 169

In the words of P Diddy, *"Don't chase the paper. Chase the dream"*. I have a dream for women and men to have no shame about money. They are empowered by making money because they know they are the global thought leaders in the world that will use that money to create change and positive growth. **I want the right people making millions** because I know they will make a difference. I know my legacy is to give people the hope of being financially free through their business and the specific formula to get there. I know my legacy is to help make millionaires that have legacies that will share that wealth to live their own abundant lives and share that with others.

Day 170

Who can I help?

Who can I serve?

I never awake without asking how can I make $10K or where will I get 3 new clients. **Clients and money come when you are in service.** Clients and money come when you are aggressively seeking ways to help.

Day 171

Realize there is a difference between wanting to serve and being of service. Wanting to serve is you are meditating, thinking, and wishing that your gift can touch people. **Being of service is leaving your house, picking up the phone, emailing, and LIVING your service.** Asking people every day to experience your work and grow from your gift.

Day 172

I was so sick of hearing of about the word niche that I thought that I was going to throw up. So I said "what is niche to me?" What does it mean to me? I've got to find a niche but I can't talk about it that way – it just feels aggressive and even sleazy at times. And then I recognized my niche, the way I would talk about it is **"who needs you most?"** What's the group of people who are yearning for your experience and your gifts to help them.

Day 173

Know that a movement can make waves.
Many of you are waiting and quite frankly
failing because you believe someone else's
opinion of you or your movement. Any
movement worth launching will have naysayers and negative reactions. **If I
stopped every time someone
disagreed with me, I would not
have a business.** If I quit each time
someone told me "I can't," I would still be in
a meaningless job. A movement makes
waves- YOU have to be willing to ride them.

Day 174

If you don't have what you want – **why are you worried about failing?**

Day 175

I have been placed on this planet at this time and surrounded by these people to leave a legacy of truth, wisdom, and abundance around money. I am aware that not all of this will be easy or quick and much of the divine plan will happen in a different way than I envisioned, but I am a legacy maker. **I have a moral obligation to leave a legacy that helps, supports, and heals** people long after I am gone. I am dedicated to my legacy.

Day 176

I am clear that abundance is my birthright. My life was meant to live in beauty, joy, pleasure, and purpose. I can have whatever I want because everything I need is present to have it. Charging little for my services or playing down the beauty of money does not serve me or my clients. Abundance is all our birthright and money is a vehicle. It is fuel for my legacy- it supports my best life, but it also allows me to support the best lives of others and have my legacy and impact reach more and be more.

Day 177

Make certain you spend more time in front of people than in front of your computer! (Especially in the growth stages.) Making those decisions of best color for your website or researching what other people in your field are doing all have their place, but they do not directly bring you the opportunity to start a client conversation.

Use the 80/20 rule. 80% of your time networking, meeting, and speaking and 20% of your time on strategy and research.

Day 178

Don't be so picky in the beginning. I hear people say they don't like this group or they are not sure if that networking organization will do anything for them. Just GO! You have no idea who someone will know or who they might be able to introduce you to. You will soon learn which groups serve you and which groups don't, but to start just go, meet, and share your movement.

Day 179

Don't have a drunk cowboy message. You know those people who you ask, "What do you do?" and 10 minutes later you are still trying to figure out what the heck they are talking about. Be clear and concise with a 2 or 3 sentence message. I call this your impact statement.

Day 180

Act like it's your party. Walk into every room as if you own it. Walk into every room as if these wonderful people have gathered here just to meet you. Greet them, be curious, ask questions, be gracious, and be in your power. People are attracted to confidence. Authority inspires.

Day 181

Follow up and ask.

Follow up with everyone you meet within 48 hours, even if it is just a quick "nice to meet you" email. Be certain to ask how you can help them and offer them a session, a freebie, or an offer to move them closer to knowing your work.

Ask for what you want, a referral, an opportunity to share how you can work with them, or an alliance/partnership.

Day 182

Make your mess your message.

Day 183

Clients generate money. That's how most of us make money. It doesn't matter if a client buys a product, or if they work with your one-on-one, or they sign up for a 6-month program. It is clients. It is people that we're looking for to generate income.

Income does not come from people.

Money does not come from people.

Money comes through people.

Day 184

The Universe will send you what you ask for. **But if you don't give it specifics it doesn't know what to provide you.**

If I'm sending someone out for lunch to bring me back lunch, and I say "oh just get me lunch." And they come back with a saltine cracker. If I say "are you crazy! I needed lunch." And they say "well you didn't tell me what."

You've got to get specific!

Day 185

Everything you need to build a multiple six-figure business is **within a one-mile radius of your home.** You can have all the websites in the world, you can have the marketing materials, you can have all of that, but if you are not talking to at least 100 people a week, then you are not reaching enough people.

Day 186

If you are talking to enough people and still not making sales, you have an authenticity problem. This means you're not bringing enough of *you* into it. When you don't bring enough of *you* into it, you either are scared to death to sell at all, or you're overselling and not being your authentic self.

Day 187

You have to track your sales.

You have to know your numbers.

You have to know your conversions.

And once you know them, **you can then work on them.**

Day 188

You have to have a **system to sell.**

Day 189

Sales is just **the opportunity** to transform someone's life.

Day 190

Mother Theresa

Buddha

Ghandi

They were the greatest sales people to have ever walked the earth. Because they knew that they were so passionate about somebody, about something that **if they got other people passionate about it they could change the world.**

Which they did!

Day 191

Don't confuse the value of money with the value of being caring. The more money you can make, the more caring you can be. The more money you make, the more you can give.

Day 192

If you can **cry** about it you can **sell it.**

Day 193

Figure out one thing you know you can do really well. And only do that one thing.

Day 194

No one ever cast a play without the script. **The script is your movement.** You decide the story line. Then you can cast the characters. And the characters are the customers and clients.

Day 195

Be willing to make a fool of yourself every day.

I remember riding the train from New Jersey to New York to my day job. I was journaling in a notebook and I thought, "Gosh, how am I going to do this?" I had bought into the mantra, "Build it and they will come," but when I first started my business, I was struggling to get clients.

And as I was writing in my notebook, this came to me:

"If I am willing to make a fool of myself every day, this is all going to work out."

Day 196

If you are willing to be the change that you want to see in the world, you are going to look a little out of the ordinary. You're going to seem a little off-center.

You may even be called crazy.

Day 197

Do what you love.

People often ask me, "How do you stay motivated to market?" **This question scares me.**

If you have to motivate yourself to market your business, you may be in the wrong business.

I put both feet on the floor in the morning, and the first thing I think about is, "Who can I help? Who can I serve?" I actually say that to myself every morning. "Who can I help? Who can I serve?" I know that I can't help or serve people without marketing, so doing what I love is paramount.

Day 198

My biggest pet peeve is that you say "I didn't get...."

You've got to ask for what you need!

Day 199

People always ask me, "How did you find the time to build your business?"

I was working a 50-60 hour weekday job in New York City while I built my business. Of course, I am no longer in that day job, but I did work that day job up until early 2009.

Time melts away when you are in a movement. Time will not melt away when you are *working*, but it will melt away if you are being the change that you want to see in the world.

When you are in love with what you're doing and it is a movement, time melts away.

Day 200

Marketing is just like breathing. **It's your moral obligation.**

Day 201

Whatever you do, **make sure it's 100% YOU!**

There is no magic formula for success. Everyone is different and you need to make sure that the business you build is authentically yours.

Day 202

Go to the YES. **It will never come to you.**

Day 203

When you love what you do... when you wake up every day feeling like if you didn't do it then it would be criminal, then you figure out, learn, and do whatever it takes.

For me money is love. It allows me to share, give, develop, and grow. Over the last three years I was never chasing the money- I was always chasing the dream.

I was chasing the love – the love I had to share with people that I knew would then turn and share with others – that deep, rich ripple effect love.

Day 204

Chasing the money doesn't work. At some point you will get bored and angry when things don't go exactly as you planned. **Money is not that hard to make. Really.** You could think of 100 ways to make money today – illegally, legally, in a job, asking, begging, Ebay, on and on. Money is not that hard to make. The hard part is making a difference. When you can make money by making a difference, everything is deeper. You don't mind the hits or jabs or naysayers that come your way, you simply keep chasing the dream because when your dream comes true, so does everyone's around you.

Day 205

I never ask how much money I can make. Don't misunderstand me. I am in this to make money – I know that money will allow me to change my world, your world, and the entire world. I just know it is not the fastest path to cash. **I know when I love people, when I serve people, and when I help people, money always follows IF I am certain to ask.** You can't just live your life giving everything away. I know that by charging the RIGHT rate for my services I help people and you do too.

Day 206

Just as most new business owners commonly do, I used to say, **"People have just given me their name, I don't want to bother them and send them things all the time."** I had to recognize that touching their lives in a meaningful way allows *the cream to rise to the top.* Those who are truly interested in what you have to say and the solutions you offer will make themselves known to you. The rest may unsubscribe or walk away from you, but that means they really weren't engaged or dedicated to your message anyway.

Day 207

Your target market is not necessarily who you work with, **it's who you market to.**

Day 208

The investments that I have made in myself never got lost in the stock market crash. No recession can ever devalue them.

Day 209

Make quick and confident decisions. Don't get stuck in limbo. Whether you're unsure about a decision to invest in a training opportunity, an event or directly in your business, don't be indecisive. Successful entrepreneurs make quick decisions.

Day 210

The more you share your message, the faster you accelerate in building the business.

Constantly ask yourself:
Where can I speak?

How can I get my writing published?

Who can I talk to?

Where can I volunteer?

On what sites can I blog?

What gatherings can I go to?

Who can I call or email?

How else can I share my message?

Day 211

No entrepreneurial vision has ever come to
fruition by being **kept a secret.** You must
to take the show on the road.

Day 212

You will **never regret** investing in yourself and your business.

Day 213

No man is an island. **Work only in your strengths** and find the people to help you do those things that are not strengths for you right now.

Day 214

I like to work with people who are experts in their areas, so I tend to work with several different virtual assistants. **I choose people who really excel in their particular field** and use them for those particular tasks and project management.

Day 215

You must from the start create a business model that supports your life and your desired freedom. If you don't, before you know it the business is going to be running you.

Day 216

You can put a positive spin on your message all day long. **But do you want to know what gets people's attention?**

"Are you broke?"

"Want to make money?"

You don't need to put a positive spin on it, it just needs to be good marketing.

And you have to be truthful.

Day 217

When you're specialized **there is no competition.**

Day 218

There are no target market police.

Make a decision.

The niche you choose may not be where you end up. But it will get you to where you're going.

It is the indecision of not choosing something and moving forward with it that stops people from ever growing a business.

Day 219

Tell stories.

Day 220

To every third grader, **a fourth grader is a God.**

Day 221

Don't be afraid to **let your panties show.**

Day 222

Marketing doesn't stop – it happens constantly.

Day 223

Don't try to change the world. **Change your world.**

Day 224

If it doesn't make sense – **stop doing it!**

Day 225

Be fearless. Even in the face of uncertainty and possible failure we do it anyway. Embracing fear is the key success component.

Day 226

You have to let go of something of a lower nature to get **something of a higher nature.**

Day 227

You don't have to be an expert in everything. Find the experts.

Day 228

Don't be a drunken sailor when telling people what you do. **If they can't understand you, they're not going to buy from you.**

Day 229

You need to know exactly what a client costs you.

Day 230

Who can I help?

Who can I serve?

What is the **fastest path to cash?**

Day 231

Don't stop!

Day 232

There are **3 ways to get more money.**

Increase your fees

Increase frequency

Increase clients

Day 233

What's the one singular piece of advice that I can give business builders that are launching a business or growing their business?

It's taking action every day – every single day.

Sometimes it's big action and sometimes it's little action. That's not what's important. It's that you're working on it in some capacity every day, and **even on the bad days.**

Day 234

Authority inspires. They can't talk about you if you can't talk about you.

Day 235

The world does not need anymore information. **It needs implementation.**

Day 236

Sometimes you just **buy a blindfold and you do it anyway.**

Day 237

They may not remember everything that you taught them. **They will never forget how you treated them.**

Day 238

A **confused mind** always says **NO.**

Day 239

Your clients **will create your business** for you in the beginning.

Day 240

If it's comfortable – it's not right.

Day 241

If you are getting a lot of YESES,
you may not be doing something right.

Day 242

If everything is under control – **you are in trouble.**

Day 243

If you're waiting for the right time, **there is none.** There is only right now.

Day 244

You can help millions, **but you can't do it until you help one first.**

Day 245

If you are in the business of helping people, you need to have a name that means something to them – **not to you.**

Day 246

If you have a **backup plan, you will ALWAYS use it.**

Day 247

What do you want?

What are you afraid of?

If there are no judgments – what would you do?

You don't need to know the 'how'.
You need to make a decision.

Day 248

Indecision is a form of self-abuse.

Day 249

Don't put yourself in a position where you empower **bad decisions.**

Day 250

Tell them what you're going to tell them.

Tell them.

Tell them what you told them.

Day 251

The fastest path to cash is always one on one client work.

Day 252

You need to coach 100 people before your ideal client will begin to crystalize.

It is in those conversations.

Day 253

Ask for support from others. They can't help you if you don't tell them what you need.

Day 254

Make a top 10 reasons sheet why someone should work with you.

Day 255

Do not hide behind the computer and technology. **Get out there!**

Day 256

The person with the most certainty always closes the sale.

Day 257

You will never make money if you have to feel special because you choose to be special over money. **If none of us cares who gets the credit, can all make money.**

Day 258

No one is a self-made millionaire.
You can't do it alone.

Day 259

How many times do we chastise people for taking out a $30,000 student loan?

You need to invest in your business just like you would invest in your education.

Day 260

You can't be stuck if you're not going anywhere.

Day 261

Money is always in the silence.
Don't talk them out of the sale.

Day 262

Do something in your business every day!

Day 263

If you don't try to sell what you have to offer to your best friends, **you don't have a business.**

Day 264

Stories sell.

Day 265

Debt

    Negative

      Positive

Any good business **requires debt.**

It is **impossible** to be in business without debt.

It needs to be good debt.

If you incur the debt you have to have a plan to pay it down.

Day 266

Don't make asking hard. Because it is the most vulnerable place you can be. **Make it easy.**

Day 267

When you get your cash flow right, it will allow you to do other things.

Day 268

Where are your **low hanging fruit?**

Day 269

"I don't have money."

Where did you sleep last night? Do you own or rent? Then you have money.

Did you eat today? Then you have money.

Let's get clear. **You DO have money.** You're response should be "I'm choosing to spend my money elsewhere."

Day 270

Are you happy with your life right now?
**You must be if you're not willing
to change.**

Day 271

Follow-up.

Follow-up.

Follow-up.

That's your job.

Day 272

What other people charge has **nothing to do with you.**

Day 273

People will always spend money
on what they're passionate about.

Day 274

When you land that first speech you may or may not be paid. No worries! **Be sure to have two things ready when you go:**

a) A way to collect all the names for your database. I suggest raffling of a month of your services, a spa basket, or a book depending on your target market.

b) Have something to offer them at a special deal if they sign up with you that evening. (i.e. your new group forming is $199 per month, but if they register today it is $149)

Day 279

You haven't finished the conversation if you haven't gotten the NO.

Day 280

What's it going to look like **if you don't get there?**

Day 281

Treat your best customers better.
Create special opportunities for higher level customers.

Day 282

Bartering always leaves someone with the short end of the stick. There is an energy exchange around money. Don't barter. You are better than that. **Pay someone for their services and get paid for yours.**

Day 283

Instead of "transitioning to the sale" and thinking that it is really difficult. Don't transition to the sale.

Instead show up in service. If they need something you have, a resource that will be useful, suggest it, and offer it to them.

Day 284

You have to establish

Know

    Like

        Trust

Day 287

It's time to stop wasting time. It is time to do what you know you want to do - build your dream business.

How much time have you already wasted thinking about getting started?

Day 288

Identifying with your market is very important because to authentically and successfully serve a specific market, you must understand and identify with the hearts of that market. **You must relate to what they are going through.** You must know the conversation going on in their head without even asking. You must embrace their story and their problem. You must genuinely care so deeply for this market that you don't want to just help them--you MUST help them.

Day 289

You aren't *trying* to help people or make money, you are just **using your own empathy and care to make a difference.**

Day 290

It is important that you are inspired by your tribe and excited to serve them, but they also **have to be viable in the market unless you are using your service for volunteer work.**

Day 291

People don't want to say No. **They would rather lie than to tell you No.**

They will check their credit cards, they will say that their cat is in chemotherapy, anything not to have to say No to you.

Society hates to tell people No.

You have to use your intuition and to be skillful in your coaching.

Be fine with them to say No.

It's not fine for them to mislead you or themselves in some kind of random story just to get out of it.

Day 292

Your truth will set them free.

What they can relate to in YOUR story or situation can often times attract the client without you doing a thing.

Day 293

You have a story that no one else has. It is unique and it is valuable for clients to understand the person behind the credentials. Credentials aren't to be left out-- they just shouldn't be the centerpiece. Take a moment to brainstorm your credentials so you can weave those into your story.

Day 294

We are all given the **same possibility.**

We are all given the **same opportunity.**

We are all on a **level playing ground.**

Day 295

I decided that **I would not worry about failing.**

Day 296

My purpose is to help people heal their shame around money and then give the marketing and mindset tools to do that.

Day 297

This may piss a lot of people off – but meditation and money don't mix.

A lot of people are believing that if they just BE, that money will come and the business will come.

Who you are being absolutely plays a role in your marketing. **But make no mistake, if you are not marketing 3 – 5 hours a day, it is not going to work.**

Period.

You have to do it.

Day 298

Overcoming your resistance to marketing...and realizing it's the fastest way to create massive change in the world...

Is pivotal to your success!

Day 299

Have a clean and clear movement message that gets people to say **"tell me more."**

Day 300

Market 3 – 5 hours a day – minimally and **automate strategies that market without you.**

Day 301

Take imperfect action on a daily basis and implement before you know all of the answers.

Day 302

Do you know what numbers you need to hit your businesses financial goals?

Day 303

You don't need to put on fancy bells or add whistles to make more money. **You actually need to go back to the basics.** Go back to what inspired you to start your business and share your gift. Go back to what you already know, have and are. Put YOU back in the process.

Day 304

Get active income going in your business ASAP. Active is where you are "doing" the work. Coaching a client, having a session, leading a group, etc.

Then you can move into passive income. Passive income is where you might sell a book, product, or program that does not involve your time. Passive income typically requires a larger list and a deeper reach. I am all for passive income–very important–but AFTER you have active income so that you are nurturing relationships, referrals, and your visibility.

Day 305

We often get so busy with the latest marketing trend that we forget to check our backyard for opportunities. Have you emailed friends, family, and associates? Have you set up coffee with people in your circle of influence? Have you had a house party and invited people over for a mini workshop or seminar? **Don't forget the opportunities from people who already know, like, and trust you.**

Day 306

Make a list of all networking and visibility opportunities within about one minute of your home. OK, if you live in the country or deep woods, maybe change this to 10 miles. Churches, schools, cafes, doctor offices, community groups...I mean seriously, do this exercise. **Get in your car and drive around for 20 minutes.** Look at everything as a potential place to speak, network, and share your business.

Day 307

Maybe getting out of the house is not that easy for you or you lie in an area that is difficult to reach civilization. **Then WRITE!** Seek out places to be a guest blogger, guest newsletter writer, article market, post on forums, and use your email like you mean it. Write about your work everywhere and anywhere you can.

Day 308

Cold Call – I know. THE. DIRTY. WORD. What I mean is cold calling with purpose. Could you call former clients and ask for referrals? Call friends and brainstorm marketing opportunities. Certainly call places to speak, from the local library to the Chamber to the associations within your market. I tell you, **making five targeted calls a day WILL grow your business.**

Day 309

Movement over Marketing. Go back to what matters. Your mission, your meaning, and your purpose IS what sells. The fastest path to authentic income is realigning with your WHY! It is what attracts people to work with you.

Day 310

Accelerating our income becomes elusive when we lose sight of the resources we already have available to us. So—breathe and take a step back. **Clients, business, and income are all around you.** Reach out and grab it so you can help more people.

Day 311

People buy solutions, not services and not a process. People are running a race because they want to make it to the finish line. They do the same thing in the marketplace for coaching. People seek solutions to their problems. That's the finish line for them. They seek answers to their dilemmas. If you package and offer solutions, you can relay a message that people understand and want.

This fact that people buy solutions not services and a process also really ties into your target market. I know for me when I shifted my message to what solutions I have for people's problems, it totally shifted my business.

Day 312

Stop waiting for everything to be ready, perfect, or right to launch your business.

My dad's a farmer and he always says, "You want to know the best way to find out that corn will grow? Plant it." You can prepare and research yourself into a corner, but at some point the seed has to hit the earth.

Day 313

From the moment I started my coach training I started my marketing training and I started marketing my business. It's one of the single most important factors to the success I have.

I didn't hold back. I jumped in and I made terrible mistakes. I launched my business anyway and it gave me momentum and it gave me some immediate results. I can tell you that an entrepreneur making money is more effective, productive and motivated than one planning to make money. That was huge for me. **Just do it anyway.**

Day 314

Think about what you cannot get enough of. What or who just fires you up and you could talk about it for days? It's the kind of thing that people have to shut you up because you're so impassioned you want to share it. **That's your target market. That's your hive. Those are the people who need you most.**

Day 315

Become Hype Free

Are you sharing the best of you and giving away the good stuff? People don't need hype and they certainly don't buy hype. Check your messages, your language, and your marketing and make sure you are providing high content, high value, and the highest level of support.

Day 316

My mentor says, "Suzanne, You must get comfortable with being uncomfortable". **Ugh.** That is so hard. I know why....I get it. My other mentor says "business is messy". So if you know that business is ever changing, can be messy, and really is an ebb and flow. You must be OK with being uncomfortable. Lots of unexpected things will happen. Lots of unknowns will be present. Lots of mistakes will take place. You sit in uncomfortable quite a bit.

Being comfortable with being uncomfortable doesn't mean you have to be out on a limb, no safety net, or reckless. It mean's you ride the big waves, go fearlessly into the ocean, and you wear a life vest.

Day 317

Unless you are a VA or web designer you should not be doing your websites, autoresponders, or admin stuff. **Get the help. Find the help. Borrow the help.** Do only what you do and the marketing.

Day 318

Know how to sell. Oh, yes...the dirty word. **Before you create programs, write material, and take 5 years of training, know how to sell.** You can not operate a business if you do not know how to sell. Business is about currency. You must ask for the client to get clients.

Day 319

To launch, grow, or makeover a business you will need to invest in yourself. Watching thousands of aspiring entrepreneurs **EVERY single one that succeeded had a mentor, attended events, and invested in themselves.** The money is always present. The Universe provides what we need, but you have to be open to it and willing to do what it takes.

Day 320

Realize next to selling the other must-have in your business is **a constant list building strategy.** You can start this today with offline and online marketing. Your job is to collect names so that you can authentically communicate your message. Collecting names builds an audience. Get some support to set up automated systems to make this happen.

Day 321

Get over being in control cause you aren't. We are in control of our thoughts and that's it. The rest is somebody else's doing, so spend the majority of your time focusing on thoughts, mindset, and mental shifts. The way we think is the way we live.

Day 322

Stop asking for so many opinions cause you know what? YOU will get them. And you will be confused as heck. If that means unsubscribing from me right now then so be it. Choose 2-3 voices and people that resonate and study them, look to them, learn from them. Your husband and best friends should not be on this list. Sorry!

Day 323

Money is not evil.

In fact, it's your primary engine for doing good in the world.

Day 324

Turn complaints into requests.
Most of the time we don't know what to do
because we are complaining; we are fretting
or we are confused. ASK. REQUEST! Every
time you find yourself complaining about
your business, give $20 to charity. Either
stop complaining or stop the business. It
doesn't work.

Day 325

Leave the damn house. 90% of you reading this work in isolation and for yourselves; get out of the house. There is a whole world out there – go explore it. If you are leaving your house where are you going? Are you surrounding yourself with the right people? Are you seeking success in a physical human connection form?

Day 326

As a coach, when you talk about "your practice", it has a definition and an insinuation of one-on-one coaching. It is important to build coaching businesses that aren't solely based on one-on-one coaching. Certainly one-on-one coaching is a component – and for some people a very large component – of their coaching business, but **you cannot build a successful business when only offering one-on-one coaching.**

Day 327

It's very important to start your marketing early. Within about nine months of starting my business, I had over 35 paying clients. My business had really boomed. Things were going really well, and in about 14 months it went to six figures.

I had no marketing background per se. I certainly had never run or operated a business before. I created a very systematic marketing process for my business. **I started early and I marketed often.**

Day 328

People don't care what you do.

People care what you can do for them.

Have you heard of the radio station WIIFM? It stands for "What's in it for me?" Most everyone has their radio station tuned to WIIFM. You must appeal to the wants and needs of your ideal clients and customers.

Day 329

When you focus on what you are passionate about, work with and serve the clients and customers who need you most, making sure to appeal to their interests with clarity, **your marketing efforts will be in full alignment with who you are and you will have eliminated the biggest barriers to success in your business.**

Day 330

Stop believing you have to do it like "they" do. You are your unique brand... grasp the ideas and approaches that work for you and resonate with you. Disregard the rest and use your voice, your gifts, and your language to market.

Day 331

Don't make it complicated. **You know how to get clients – ASK.** Remember that you have traveled this path before. Look to your current circle: friends, family, colleagues, and community. Ask them to have a complimentary session with you, send a referral, or share a gift certificate with a friend.

Day 332

Draw on your past success for the present. Remind yourself of what has worked in the past and leverage that. How did you get that client? Where did those referrals come from? And what brought in money before? Repeat success.

Day 333

Just because the sun went down doesn't mean you forget your marketing sense and abandon your inner voice. Your marketing success and your authentic message is within you already...you know what your path is. Embrace your intuition to be ready for what life throws you. **That inner voice will navigate you through the business waters- even in the dark.**

Day 334

I came up with 100 ways that I could market, anything I could think of. Some of them were absolutely ridiculous, some of them were to stand on the street corner and scream at people. But some of them were

great ideas. Go to an expo, go to a Chamber meeting this week, send an email to all of my friends that I'm looking for speaking gigs. Whatever it was, I put it on that list. That's a little secret I use. It sounds like a really simple idea and technique, but I'm telling you that it has **saved me more times than you can imagine** and it never allowed me to have the excuse of, "I don't know what I can do today," because I can always pull out my list and come up with something.

Day 335

For my business to be successful I must
have a model that makes money.

Day 336

No business was ever built on uncertainty and no leader appeared out of doubt.

Day 337

The only person responsible for OUR success is US.

Day 338

Be aware that you **can't help everyone.**

Not every person may be a fit for you.

Not every person will be ready.

Day 339

Love all. Love the client relationships that work. Love the ones that don't.

Day 340

There's nothing that I hate more than going to someone's website or reading their marketing materials and reading a bio. Everybody goes, "But I'm supposed to have a bio on my website. I'm supposed to have an 'About Me' on my website."

Bios are credentials and, for the most part, pretty boring. What is fascinating, what enables you to connect with someone and enables you to really care about someone and discover empathy, is when you tell your story. This is so vitally important when you are building relationships with potential clients.

Don't tell the Cinderella version, tell the ugly step-sister, the warped version. **It is your mistakes** that really are going to leverage your clients to their own success.

Day 341

Research places to speak. I would often carve out 2-3 hours a day of "Google" time to research organizations, opportunities, and groups in my area to speak. Here is an example:

If you are a career coach for women and you live in Raleigh, NC you might Google the following: Women's organizations, career associations, churches, social clubs all in NC.

Any possible place women gather who have jobs. In the beginning it might feel vague and that is ok- get your foot in the door. Remember you will need to **contact 6-7 people to get one** booking or opportunity. Do a lot of research and make a big list. Keep carving away at that list daily.

Day 342

Don't be a character. The best way to speak is from the heart. Don't try to be over professional or perfect. People enjoy being inspired by people they can relate to. **Have fun, bring your personality out, and tell your story.** Have a good time.

Day 343

Speaking can build your list fast, get people to know-like-trust you on the spot, and you can close the sale without selling. So, go speak!

Day 344

Your income is directly tied to your environment. Take a pause. Look around you right now. Also, quickly jot down the 5 people you spend the most time with. The space you create for yourself is the mirror to your income and business potential.

Day 345

Our income, our environment, and our business are all based in choices. You can turn your environment, and thus your income, around just as quickly as you turn a light switch on or off. I have often found that when I feel a bit stuck in marketing or business growth, I really need to be working on my surroundings. I need to be up-leveling. **And yes, anytime we move ourselves into more abundance, joy, and beauty, we must leave something behind.** We always exchange something of a lower nature for a higher nature. So, maybe you don't need to be marketing this week. Maybe you need to be expanding the potential of the space and people around you.

Day 346

We are the average of the 5 people we spend the most time with. I know this can be difficult. We have best friends and family and loved ones, **but the time spent with those NOT stretching you keeps you stuck.** You may need to let some people go or just bring more abundant, juicy, positive people into your life. When you up-level the people around you, your income and joy will up-level. Remember the Rule of 5.

Day 347

Stop to smell the Roses. We often forget the smell sense and how it can have a massive effect on our mood and energy. I love Young Living Essential Oils and I can take my mind, motivation, and mojo anywhere fast by shifting the sense of smell. My favorites are Lavender, Peace and Calming, Envision, and Peppermint. Remember everything we breathe, taste, touch, or see effects our earnings.

Day 348

Flowers are luxurious and they can change the mood of any space...maybe you want fresh flowers on your desk or you position your office so that you can see flowers or trees outside. **Either way- your confidence is raised when you see beauty because you feel beautiful.** Is your office and work space beautiful?

Day 349

Travel first class. Air, hotel, meals. I know you might say, "THAT is not where I can spend my money right now" and believe me, I know what you mean...I thought that was a luxury reserved for millionaires and billionaires, but I discovered that it actually doesn't cost THAT much more and it has changed my life. I can travel with ease and no matter where I go, my surroundings remain abundant and exciting. When you up-level, your income up-levels every time.

Day 350

Provide all that we can to change people's lives and businesses.

More support

More help

More love

More gratitude

More accountability

Keep providing **MORE**.

Day 351

Gratitude. Take time in every transaction and with every client to be thankful.

Day 352

Treat every client, customer, and subscriber with the same high level of support, service, and love **no matter what package or program they participate in.**

Day 353

Own it. We are 100% responsible for all that happens at http://www.helpmorepeople.com. The good, the bad, wins, losses, mistakes, and opportunities. Own all of it.

Day 354

Be a **model** for those we serve by never giving up, always learning, and supporting people unconditionally.

Day 355

Think Big. Playing small does not serve anyone. We can only help more people if we are raising our standards, our vision, and our own bar for success.

Day 356

Play. What's the point of anything if not fully, deeply, and richly enjoyed. Play more!

Day 357

Ask. Always ask what our clients and customers want. Be on a continual quest to over serve.

Day 358

Honesty. Tell the truth even when it loses us money, time, or resources. Be an open company that values integrity.

Day 359

How are you closing the sale?
Most helpingpreneurs do this with a
complimentary session which is fine, but
calling it complimentary says- free, no pay,
low value. How about spicing it up a bit?
When I changed mine to a Laser Business
Strategy Session and added a required form
to send in prior to the call, it made a much
bigger impact on my conversion of sales and
because it was clear and focused, the client
got more out of it. What could you re-name
your sessions or replace your sessions with
that has more impact?

Day 360

Check your benefits. Remember your greatest asset is the benefits and values you bring to people. It might be time to redesign your packages and offerings. Is there a "wow" factor item you can add? Something no one else in your industry is offering that brings a punch to your packages? Jazzing up what you offer can reinvigorate your "bait" and your energy in what you deliver.

Day 361

Feeling behind? **Stop and take stock.**
Can you really be behind in business?
Whose rules are you following? This is a
great time to look at your goals, give your
vision board a makeover, or start a treasure
map. This is your business, your life, your
mission. You are only behind if you are
doing it someone else's way. Look straight
ahead.

Day 362

Be grateful. **You simply cannot feel competitive, angry, or envious if you are in a state of gratefulness.** I just grab a sheet of paper and go- set a time for 10 minutes and write gratefuls until the time is up and it simply changes your entire perspective. Look straight ahead.

Day 363

You can't help more people looking left and right. **Stay on purpose-** look ahead and keep changing the world!

Day 364

You have to **believe** in what you offer to sell what you offer. It is the self doubt and shyness about sharing our gifts that most often keeps our rates low and new clients at bay. Every marketing tool in the world is useless without a deep knowledge and understanding that you can make a difference, what you do is needed and the gifts you have MUST be shared.

Day 365

Belief is when you must share what you do. You wake up in the morning and are compelled to market because your message is that important. Your ability to change outcomes is that powerful. You must embrace the knowing that people need you, they are waiting, this is your time. When you believe, your clients believe. When you believe, new clients see that and want more. **When you believe, people are attracted to you and good comes through you.** When you believe, marketing becomes natural and just flows.

Bonus
Day 366
(perhaps it's a Leap Year)

Please don't wait to share your gifts and help more people. **We all need you.**

Thank you so much for reading **Decision Time!** This book is a capsule of the most important discoveries I made in my journey **"From Secretary to Multiple 7-Figures."**

But there is only so much I can include in a book. I want to give you even more keys to the massive impact you can have ... not only on your clients and customers. But the world!

So I have a very special gift for you!

An exclusive **free video** that reveals decision secrets that can have the biggest impact on your bottom line. Plus ongoing free powerful weekly tips, resources and offers that I make only to those who are committed to success and making a difference.

Sound good? Then pop on over to this very special page. And make the decision to have the business you have always dreamed of:

www.decisiontimebonus.com

Love,

Suzanne